Life in the Time of

Pocahontas
and the
Early Colonies

Heinemann Library
Chicago, Illinois

© 2008 Heinemann Library
a division of Reed Elsevier Inc.
Chicago, Illinois

Customer Service **888-454-2279**

Visit our website at **www.heinemannlibrary.com**

Designed by Kimberly R. Miracle and Betsy Wernert.
Printed in China by South China Printing.

11 10 09 08 07
10 9 8 7 6 5 4 3 2 1

Library of Congress Cataloging-in-Publication Data
Trumbauer, Lisa, 1963-
  Pocahontas and the early colonies / Lisa Trumbauer.
      p. cm. -- (Life in the time of)
  Includes bibliographical references and index.
  ISBN 978-1-4034-9666-9 (hc) -- ISBN 978-1-4034-9674-4 (pb)
  1. Pocahontas, d. 1617--Juvenile literature. 2. Powhatan
women--Biography--Juvenile literature. 3. Powhatan Indians--History. 4.
Jamestown (Va.)--History--Juvenile literature. 5.
Virginia--History--Colonial period, ca. 1600-1775--Juvenile literature. I.
Title.
  E99.P85.P687 2007
  975.5'01092--dc22
  [B]
                              2006102471

Acknowledgments
The author and publishers are grateful to the following for permission to reproduce copyright material: **p. 5** The Bridgeman Art Library/Private Collection/Ken Welsh, **p. 7** The British Library, **p. 8** Getty Images/MPI, **p. 9** Corbis, **p. 10** Corbis/Christie's Images, **p. 12** Corbis/Bettman, **p. 13** Getty Images/Stock Montage, **p. 14** Getty Images/ Photographer's Choice, **p. 15** Corbis/David Muench, **p. 16** Getty Images/MPI, **p. 17** Corbis/Bettman, **p. 18** North Wind Picture Archives/North Wind, **p. 19** Scala London/Art Resource/New York Public Library, **p. 20** Corbis/zefa/ Helmut Meyer zur Capellen, **p. 21** Getty Images/MPI, **p. 22** Getty Images/MPI, **p. 23** North Wind Picture Archives/ North Wind, **p. 24** Getty Images/MPI, **p. 25** The Bridgeman Art Library/Private Collection, **p. 26** The Bridgeman Art Library/Peabody Essex Museum, Salem, Massachusetts, USA, **p. 27** The Art Archive/Culver Pictures.

Map illustrations on page 4, 6, and 11 by Mapping Specialists, Ltd.

Cover photograph of engraving of Pocahontas reproduced with permission of Corbis. Cover photograph of the founding of the colony of Jamestown reproduced with permission of The Bridgeman Art Library/Private Collection.

Every effort has been made to contact copyright holders of any material reproduced in this book. Any omissions will be rectified in subsequent printings if notice is given to the publisher.

Contents

Some words are shown in bold, **like this**. You can find out what they mean by looking in the glossary.

Meet Pocahontas

Pocahontas was a Native American princess. Native Americans are people who first lived in **North America**. Pocahontas's father was a Native American chief named Powhatan. Pocahontas and her father lived with other members of the Powhatan **tribe**.

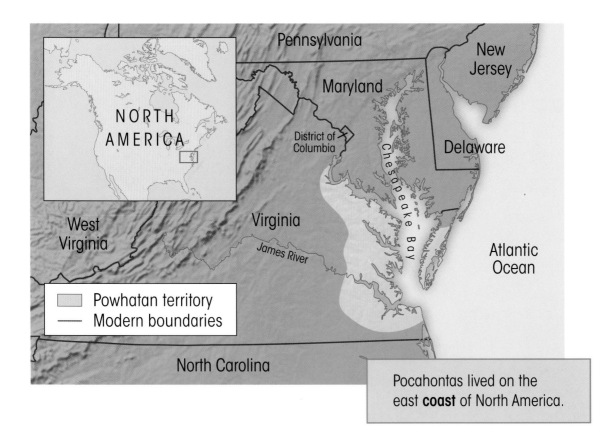

Pocahontas lived on the east **coast** of North America.

Pocahontas was 11 years old when people from England arrived in 1607.

Pocahontas's real name was Matoaka. Pocahontas was her nickname. It means "Little Wanton," or little playful one. Pocahontas was born around 1596. In 1607 her life changed when people from England arrived in North America.

Before the United States

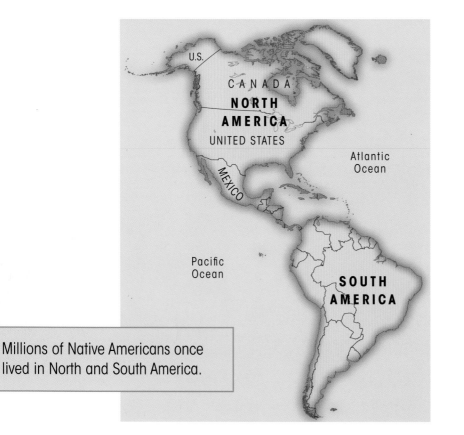

U.S.

C A N A D A

**NORTH
AMERICA**

UNITED STATES

MEXICO

Atlantic
Ocean

Pacific
Ocean

**SOUTH
AMERICA**

Millions of Native Americans once
lived in North and South America.

The United States is the name of a country. The
United States is a country on the **continent** of **North
America**. A continent is a very large piece of land.
North America has three large countries: Canada, the
United States, and Mexico.

Native Americans used things found in nature for food and clothing.

Pocahontas was born before the United States existed. Native Americans lived within their own groups (also called tribes or nations). They followed their own **traditions**. They had lived this way for hundreds of years.

Coming by Ship

Europeans are people who live on the **continent** of Europe. Europe is made of many countries. Europeans began coming to America before Pocahontas was born. They sailed to America across the Atlantic Ocean.

Europeans came to America in 1492.

England is an island that is part of Europe. In December of 1606, three ships left England for America. The ships carried about 100 men and boys. The ships arrived in America in April of 1607.

The three ships that sailed to America were the *Discovery*, the *Godspeed*, and the *Susan Constant*.

The Colony of Jamestown

James I was the king
of England in 1607.

The ships didn't stop on the **coast**. They followed a
river that led them deeper into the land. Pocahontas
and her people called this river the Powhatan. The
English **settlers** named the river the James River.

The ships traveled on the river for about three weeks. They stopped in May when they found a place to build their **settlement**. They named their settlement Jamestown, after their king.

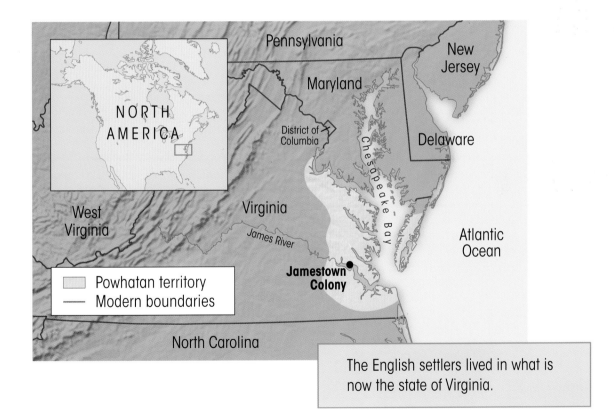

The English settlers lived in what is now the state of Virginia.

Building Shelter

The first shelter was called James Fort.

One of the first things the **settlers** needed to do was build a **shelter**. The shelter would **protect** them from the weather. The shelter would also protect them from Native Americans.

Building the shelter was not easy. Many of the men at Jamestown were **wealthy**, and in England servants did hard work for them. A settler named John Smith ordered the settlers to build James **Fort**.

John Smith became the leader of James Fort.

Finding Food

The Jamestown **settlers** also needed food. They had planned to plant spring **crops**, but it was now too late. The crops would not be ripe by the fall. The cold winter would kill the crops.

Many foods, such as corn and pumpkins, are picked in the fall.

The James River was a good place to find food.

The forests and river around Jamestown were full of animals and plants. The Jamestown settlers were not good hunters. They did not know how to fish. They did not know which forest plants were good to eat.

Trading with Powhatan

The **settlers** at Jamestown were very hungry. John Smith asked the Native Americans for help. He traded with the Native Americans. He gave them tools and they gave him food.

The settlers traded with the Native Americans.

Pocahontas and John Smith became friends.

Pocahontas often visited James **Fort**. She brought messages from her father. She also brought food for trading. The settlers liked Pocahontas and were not afraid of her.

Not an Easy Life

Jamestown was not an easy place to live. The water around Jamestown was not good for drinking. The water made the men and boys sick. Many men and boys died because of the water.

By the end of the summer of 1607, many of the settlers had died from illness.

Attacks from the Native Americans also killed some **settlers**. The Native Americans were afraid of the settlers. They were afraid the settlers would take away their lands. They didn't like the settlers living there.

The settlers lived where Native Americans had once lived, hunted, and fished.

Another Danger—Fire!

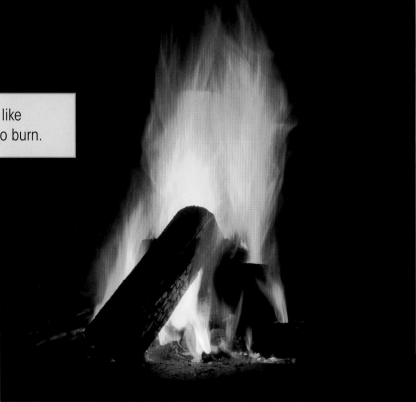

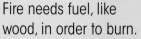
Fire needs fuel, like wood, in order to burn.

Fire was important to the **settlers**. The settlers needed fire to cook. They needed fire to keep them warm in the cold winter. Fire also gave them light inside of buildings.

The Jamestown fire destroyed most of the buildings.

In January of 1608, a huge fire spread through James **Fort**. Nearly all the buildings were burned to the ground. The settlers had to build their **shelters** again. It was winter and not the best time to start building.

More Settlers Arrive

In January of 1608, right before the fire, another ship came from England. More **settlers** arrived at Jamestown. They brought much needed supplies and food. These supplies and food helped the settlers **survive** the winter.

Two women were among the second group of settlers.

Jamestown grew bigger and bigger.

Living in Jamestown was still not easy. That didn't stop the **settlement** from growing. More ships arrived in 1609. The ships brought more supplies and more settlers.

Colonists and Native Americans

Jamestown was the first **settlement** in the English **colony** of Virginia. People who lived in the colony were called colonists. The colonists and the Native Americans did not always get along.

Sometimes the colonists and the Native Americans fought.

The colonists and the Native Americans tried to learn about each other.

Even so, the Native Americans helped the colonists. They taught the colonists how to plant and **harvest** corn. They showed the colonists how to build fish traps. They traded with the colonists.

More Colonies Are Built

Colonists on the *Mayflower* settled in Plymouth, Massachusetts in 1620.

Jamestown was the first English **colony**. It was not the last. People from England wanted to come to America. England wanted to set up more colonies in America.

It was a difficult time for Pocahontas and the Native Americans. The English took more and more land away from them. The English built **settlements** along the east **coast** of America. The English would set up 13 colonies in all.

The English **settlers** and the Native Americans tried to share the land.

If You Grew Up Long Ago

If you grew up in the time of Pocahontas…

- You would have to build your own house without any machines to help you.

- You would not have tractors to help you plant **crops**.

- You would not have refrigerators to keep your food cold and fresh.

- You would have to find ways to stay warm in the winter because your house would not have a heater.

- You would not have modern medicine to help you when you are sick.

Timeline

1492 Europeans arrive in America.

Around 1596 Pocahontas is born.

1606 Three ships leave England for America.

1607 The three ships arrive in the Virginia **colony**. They build James **Fort**, which becomes Jamestown.

1608 More ships arrive from England; a fire nearly destroys Jamestown.

1609 More ships arrive from England.

1617 Pocahontas dies.

1620 The *Mayflower* arrives in Plymouth, Massachusetts.

Find Out More

Books

Polette, Nancy. *Pocahontas*. New York: Children's Press, 2003.

Ruffin, Fraces E. *Jamestown*. Milwaukee, WI: Gareth Stevens, 2006.

Williams, Suzanne Morgan. *Powhatan Indians*. Chicago: Heinemann Library, 2003.

Zemlicka, Shannon. *Pocahontas*. Minneapolis, MN: Lerner, 2002.

Websites

Library of Congress Kids – Amazing Americans

http://www.americaslibrary.gov/cgi-bin/page.cgi/aa/all/pocahonta

Library of Congress Kids – Colonial America

http://www.americaslibrary.gov/cgi-bin/page.cgi/jb/colonial

Glossary

attack try to hurt someone by fighting

coast land next to the ocean

colony place that has been settled by people from another country

continent one of seven very large pieces of land on Earth

crop plant grown for food and other uses

fort strong building, built to protect people from attack

harvest pick or gather crops

North America one of the seven continents on Earth

protect keep safe from danger

settlement place where a group of people make a home

settler person who makes a home in a new place

shelter place to stay safe from the weather

survive stay alive

tradition custom and belief passed down from parents to children

tribe group of people who live in the same place and share traditions

wealthy having a lot of money

Index